CONTENTS

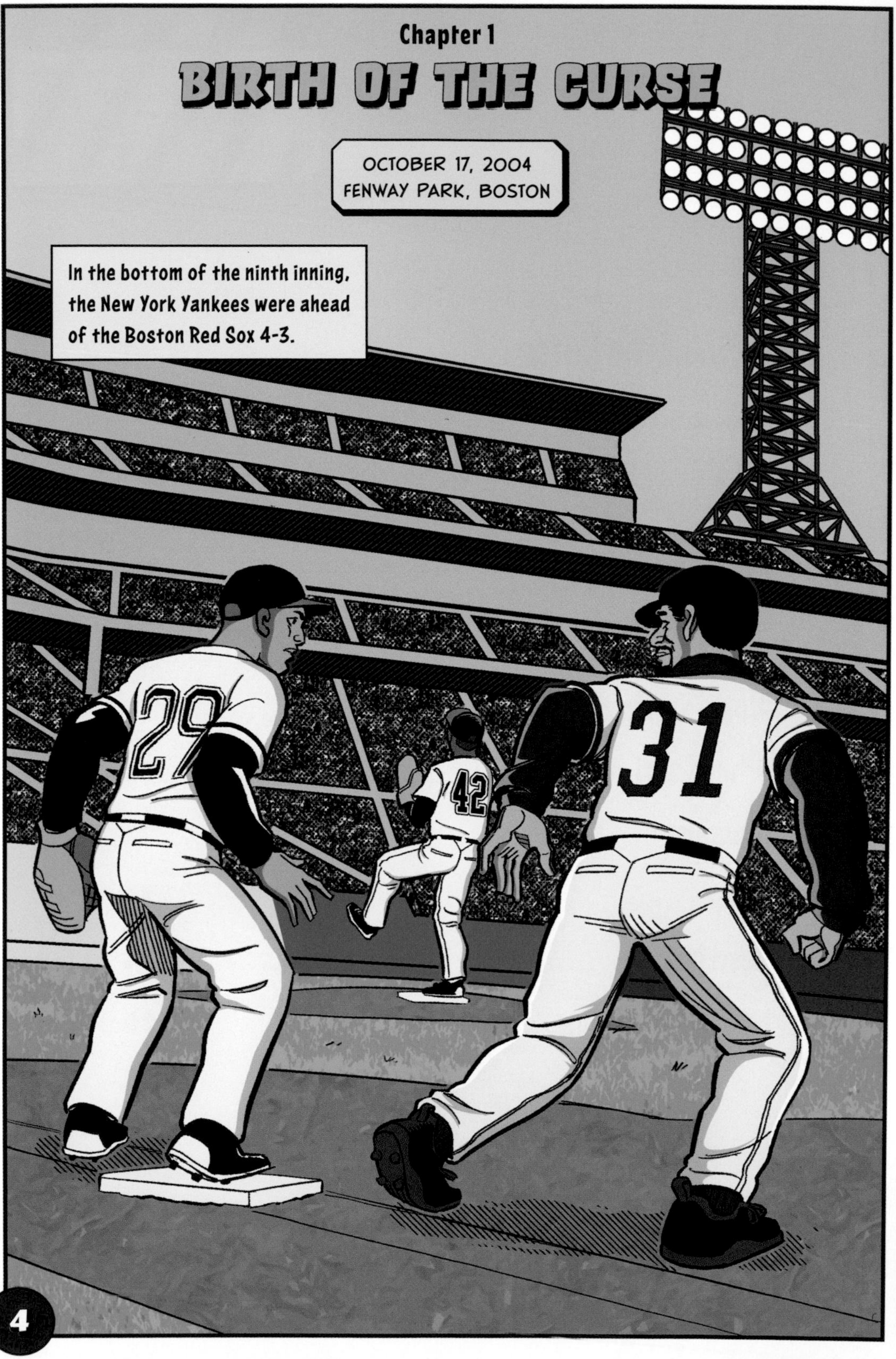

Chapter 1
BIRTH OF THE CURSE
OCTOBER 17, 2004 FENWAY PARK, BOSTON
In the bottom of the ninth inning, the New York Yankees were ahead of the Boston Red Sox 4-3.
29
42
31

AMAZING MOMENTS IN SPORTS

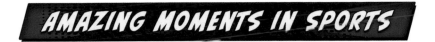

CURSE of the Bambino!

The Boston Red Sox in the 2004 World Series

RED
SOX

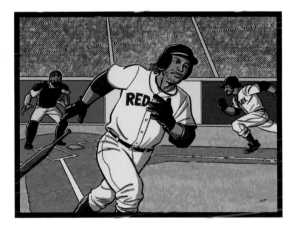

By James Buckley Jr.
Illustrated by Tom Rogers

BEARPORT PUBLISHING
Minneapolis, Minnesota

BEAR CLAW

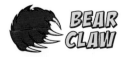

Credits

Cover art by Tom Rogers. Photos: 21 top left Courtesy Library of Congress; 21 top right courtesy Erik Drost/ Wikimedia; 21 bottom © John J. Kim/TNS/Newscom; 22 bottom via Shoreline Publishing Group.

Bearport Publishing Company Product Development Team
President: Jen Jenson; Director of Product Development: Spencer Brinker; Managing Editor: Allison Juda; Associate Editor: Naomi Reich; Senior Designer: Colin O'Dea; Associate Designer: Elena Klinkner; Associate Designer: Kayla Eggert; Product Development Specialist: Anita Stasson

Produced by Shoreline Publishing Group LLC
Santa Barbara, California
Designer: Patty Kelley
Editorial Director: James Buckley Jr.

DISCLAIMER: This graphic story is a dramatization based on true events. It is intended to give the reader a sense of the narrative rather than a presentation of actual details as they occurred.

Library of Congress Cataloging-in-Publication Data

Names: Buckley, James, Jr., 1963- author. | Rogers, Tom (Illustrator), illustrator.
Title: Curse of the Bambino! : the Boston Red Sox in the 2004 World Series / by James Buckley Jr. ; illustrated by Tom Rogers.
Description: Minneapolis, MN : Bearport Publishing Company, [2024] | Series: Amazing moments in sports | Includes bibliographical references and index.
Identifiers: LCCN 2023005604 (print) | LCCN 2023005605 (ebook) | ISBN 9798885099899 (library binding) | ISBN 9798888221716 (paperback) | ISBN 9798888223048 (ebook)
Subjects: LCSH: Boston Red Sox (Baseball team)--History--Juvenile literature. | World Series (Baseball) (2004)--Juvenile literature. | Ruth, Babe, 1895-1948--Juvenile literature.
Classification: LCC GV875.B62 B94 2024 (print) | LCC GV875.B62 (ebook) | DDC 796.357/64/0974461--dc23/ eng/20230209
LC record available at https://lccn.loc.gov/2023005604
LC ebook record available at https://lccn.loc.gov/2023005605

For more information, write to Bearport Publishing, 5357 Penn Avenue South, Minneapolis, MN 55419.

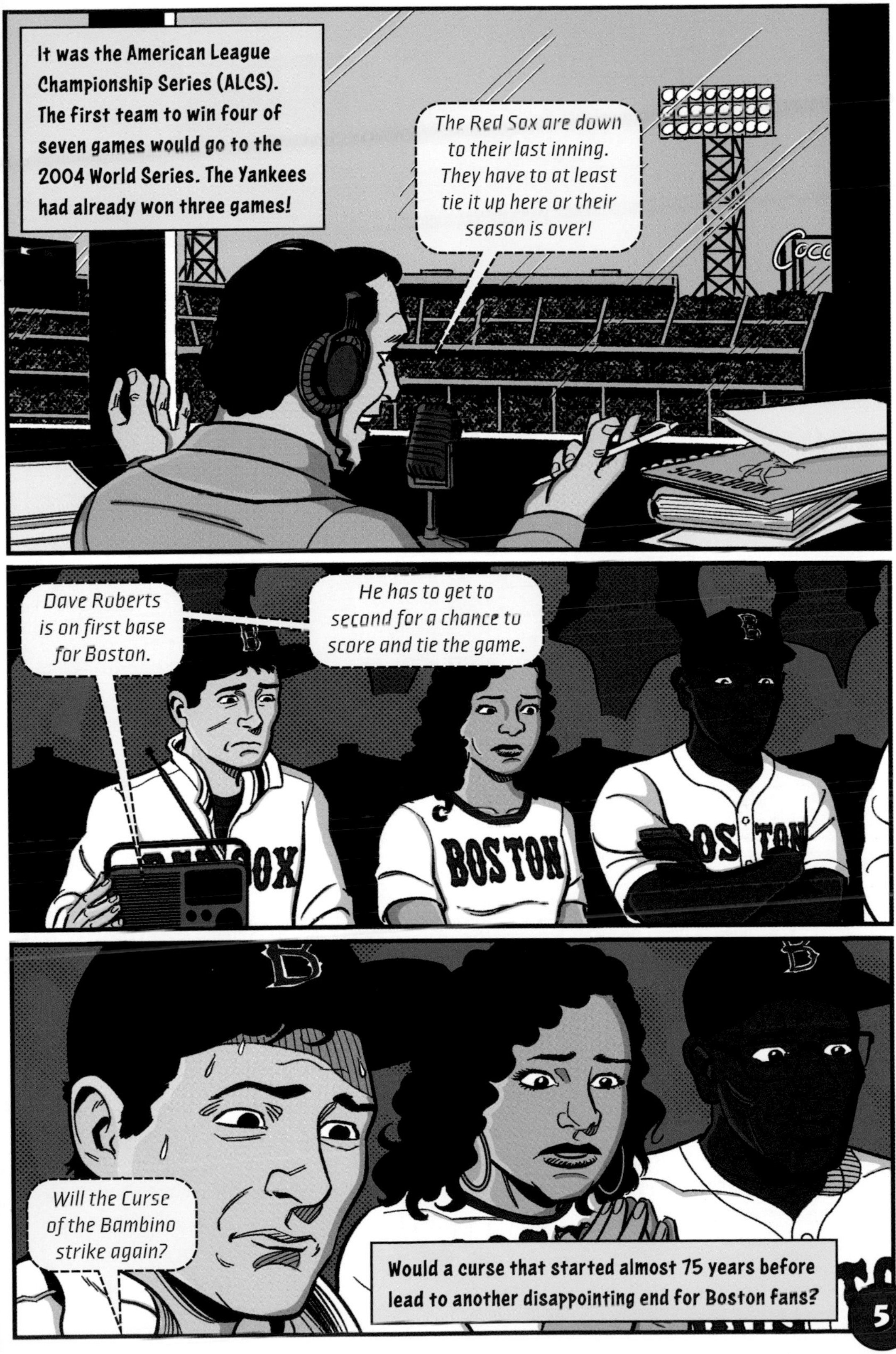
It was the American League Championship Series (ALCS). The first team to win four of seven games would go to the 2004 World Series. The Yankees had already won three games!
The Red Sox are down to their last inning. They have to at least tie it up here or their season is over!
SCOREBOOK
Dave Roberts is on first base for Boston.
He has to get to second for a chance to score and tie the game.
BOSTON
Will the Curse of the Bambino strike again?
Would a curse that started almost 75 years before lead to another disappointing end for Boston fans?

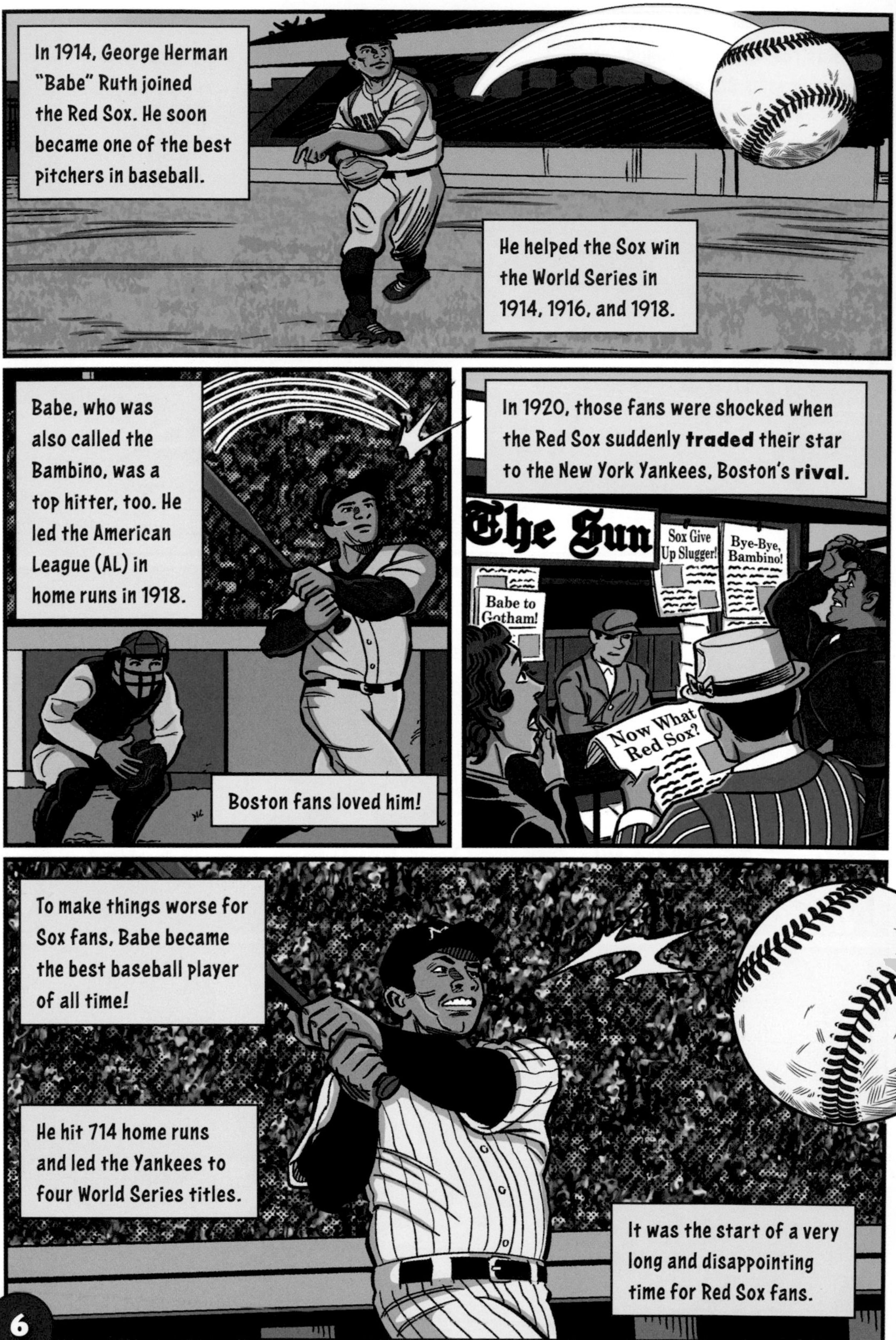
In 1914, George Herman "Babe" Ruth joined the Red Sox. He soon became one of the best pitchers in baseball.
He helped the Sox win the World Series in 1914, 1916, and 1918.
Babe, who was also called the Bambino, was a top hitter, too. He led the American League (AL) in home runs in 1918.
Boston fans loved him!
In 1920, those fans were shocked when the Red Sox suddenly traded their star to the New York Yankees, Boston's rival.
The Sun
Sox Give Up Slugger!
Bye-Bye, Bambino!
Babe to Gotham!
Now What Red Sox?
To make things worse for Sox fans, Babe became the best baseball player of all time!
He hit 714 home runs and led the Yankees to four World Series titles.
It was the start of a very long and disappointing time for Red Sox fans.

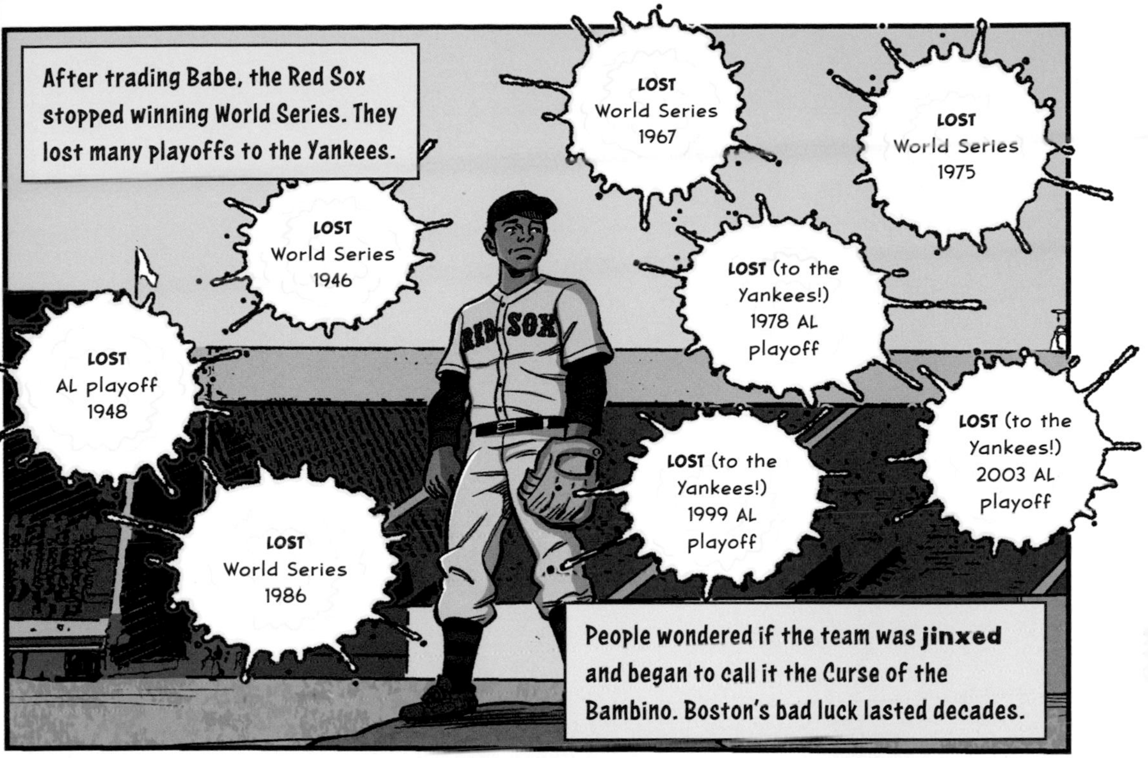

After trading Babe, the Red Sox stopped winning World Series. They lost many playoffs to the Yankees.
LOST World Series 1967
LOST World Series 1975
LOST World Series 1946
LOST (to the Yankees!) 1978 AL playoff
LOST AL playoff 1948
LOST (to the Yankees!) 2003 AL playoff
LOST (to the Yankees!) 1999 AL playoff
LOST World Series 1986
RED SOX
People wondered if the team was **jinxed** and began to call it the Curse of the Bambino. Boston's bad luck lasted decades.

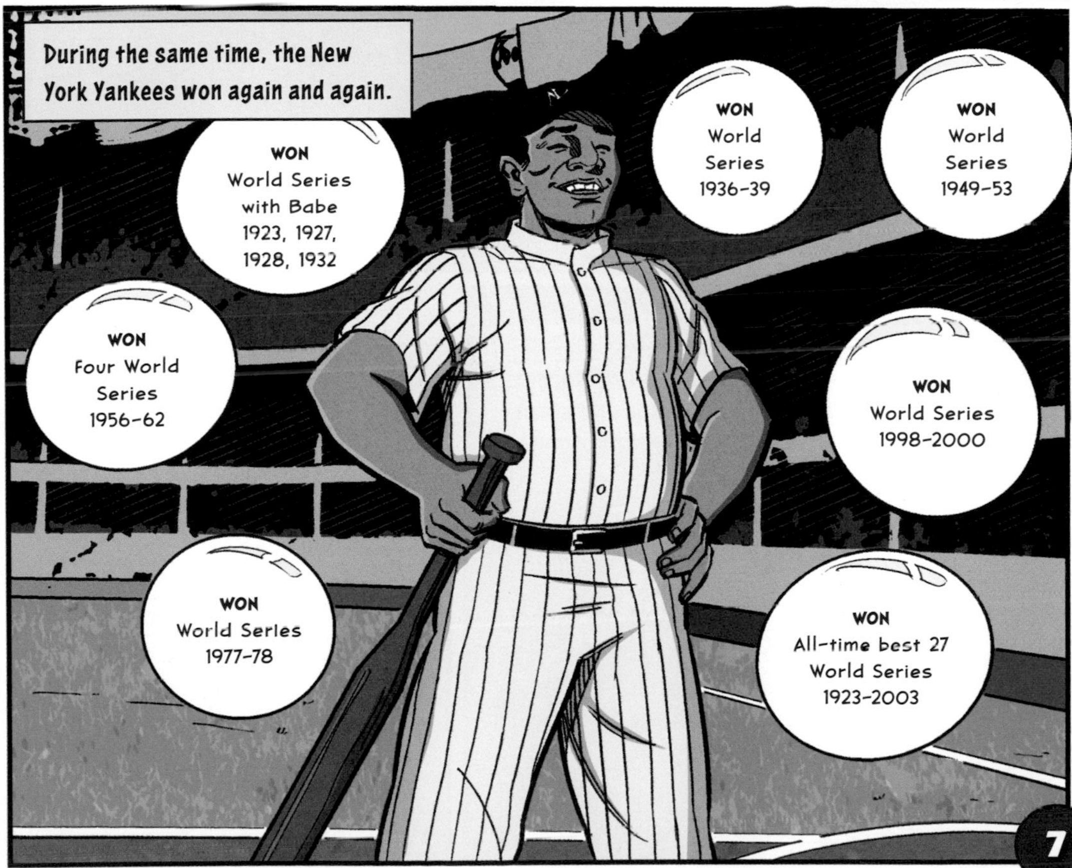

During the same time, the New York Yankees won again and again.
WON World Series with Babe 1923, 1927, 1928, 1932
WON World Series 1936–39
WON World Series 1949–53
WON Four World Series 1956–62
WON World Series 1998–2000
WON World Series 1977–78
WON All-time best 27 World Series 1923–2003

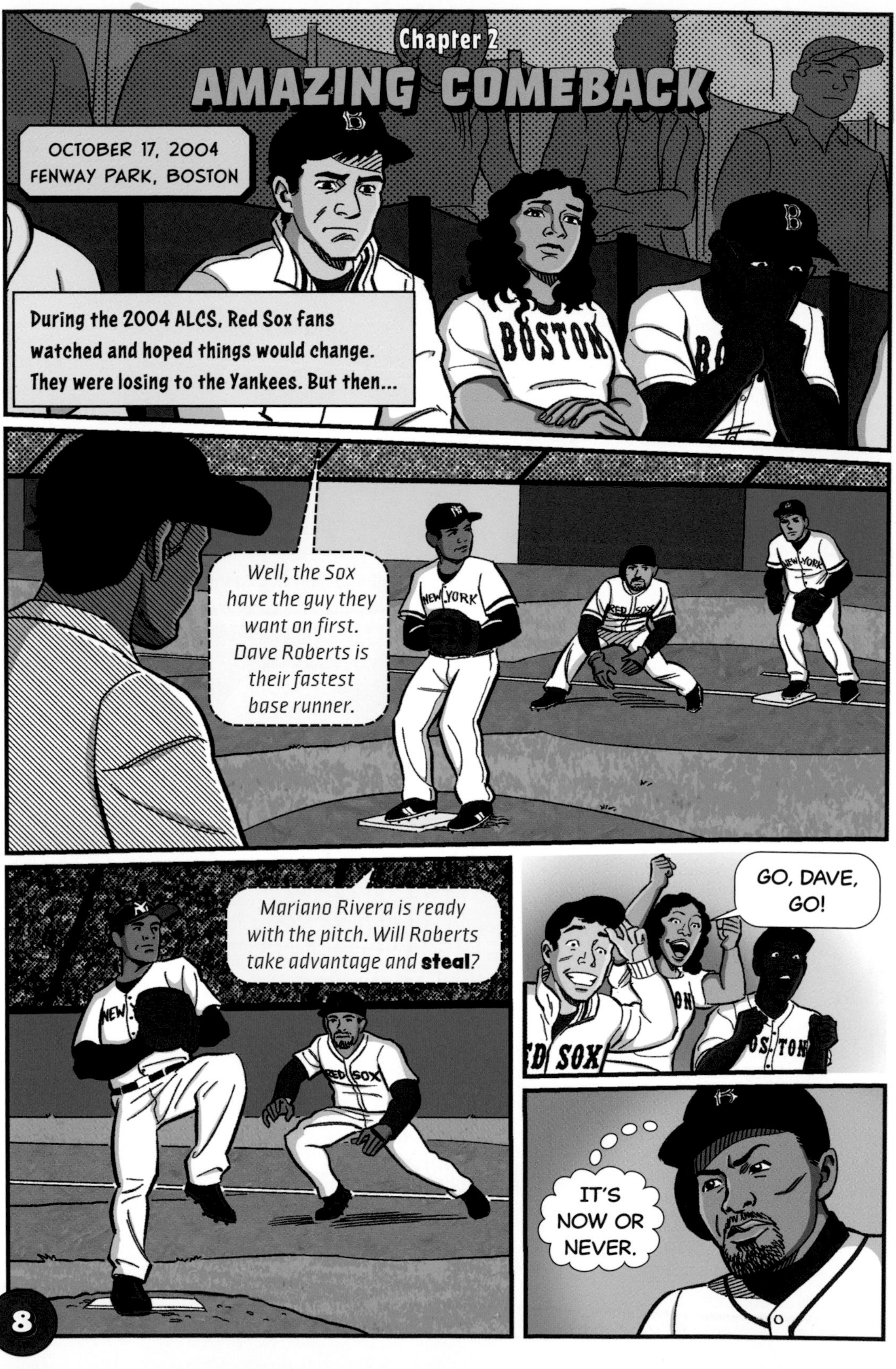
Chapter 2
AMAZING COMEBACK
OCTOBER 17, 2004
FENWAY PARK, BOSTON
During the 2004 ALCS, Red Sox fans watched and hoped things would change. They were losing to the Yankees. But then...
Well, the Sox have the guy they want on first. Dave Roberts is their fastest base runner.
Mariano Rivera is ready with the pitch. Will Roberts take advantage and **steal**?
GO, DAVE, GO!
IT'S NOW OR NEVER.

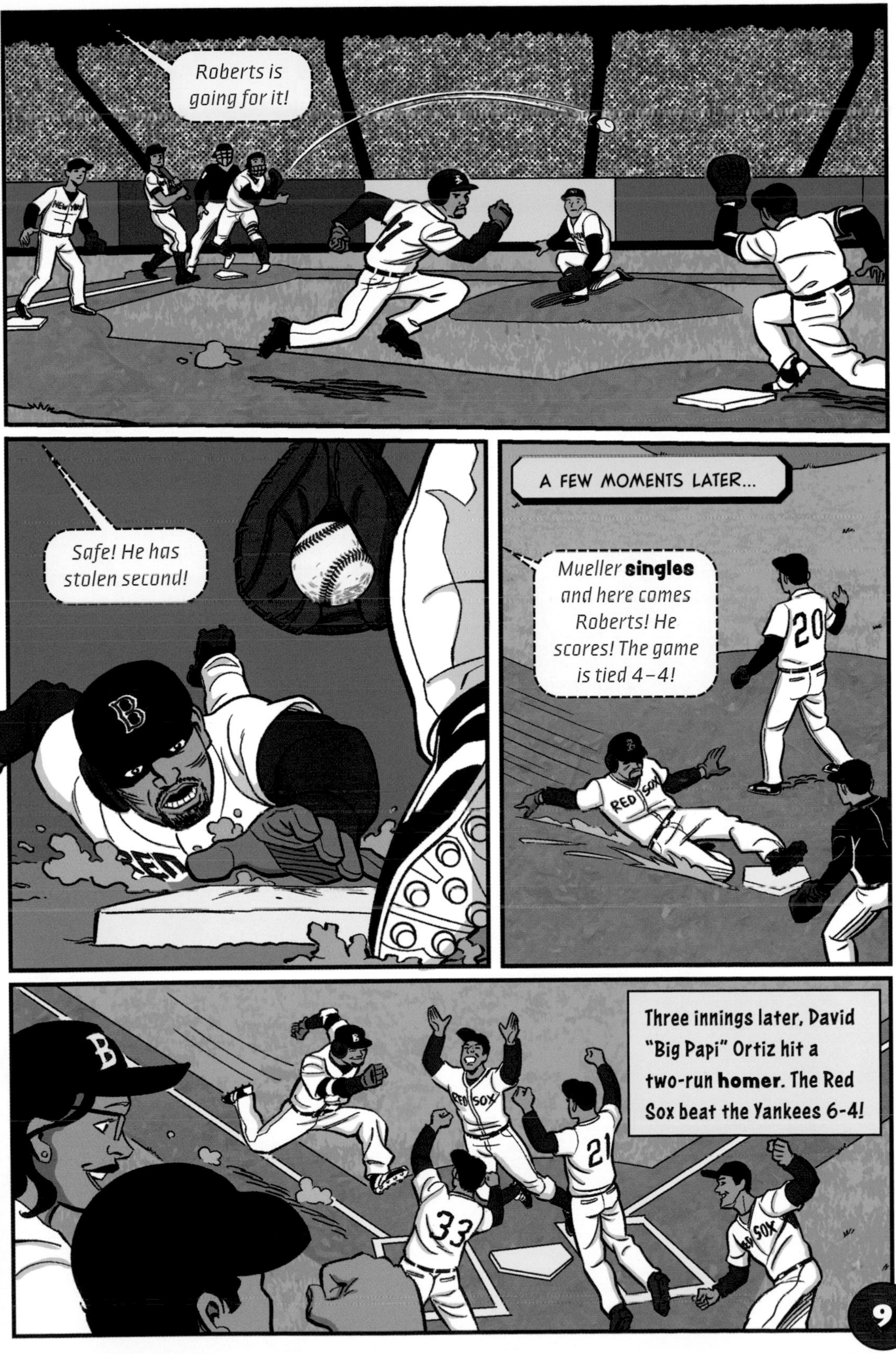
Roberts is going for it!
Safe! He has stolen second!
A FEW MOMENTS LATER...
Mueller **singles** and here comes Roberts! He scores! The game is tied 4–4!
Three innings later, David "Big Papi" Ortiz hit a two-run **homer**. The Red Sox beat the Yankees 6-4!

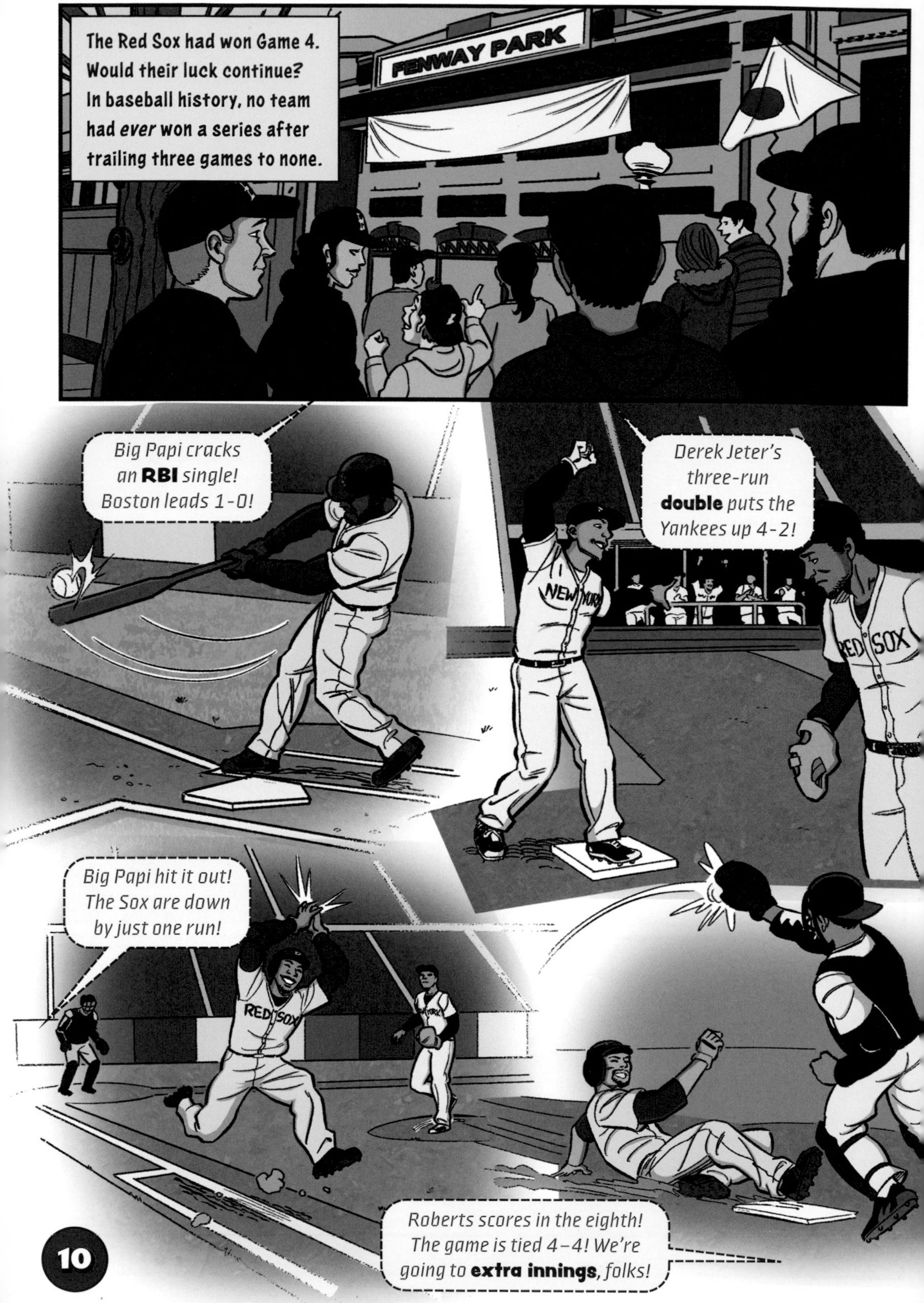
The Red Sox had won Game 4. Would their luck continue? In baseball history, no team had *ever* won a series after trailing three games to none.
FENWAY PARK
Big Papi cracks an **RBI** single! Boston leads 1-0!
Derek Jeter's three-run **double** puts the Yankees up 4-2!
NEW YORK
RED SOX
Big Papi hit it out! The Sox are down by just one run!
RED SOX
NEW YORK
Roberts scores in the eighth! The game is tied 4–4! We're going to **extra innings**, folks!

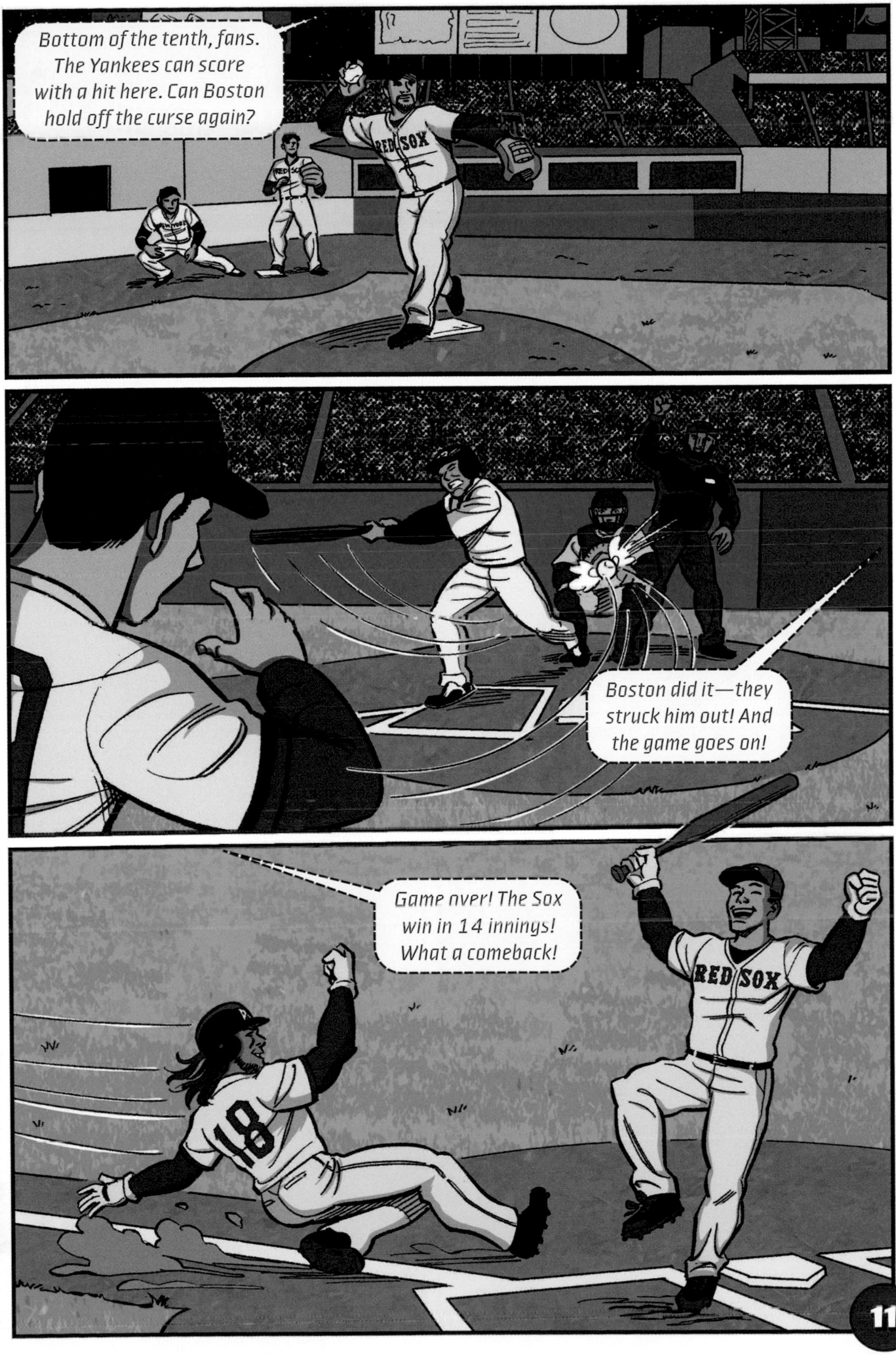
Bottom of the tenth, fans. The Yankees can score with a hit here. Can Boston hold off the curse again?
Boston did it—they struck him out! And the game goes on!
Game over! The Sox win in 14 innings! What a comeback!

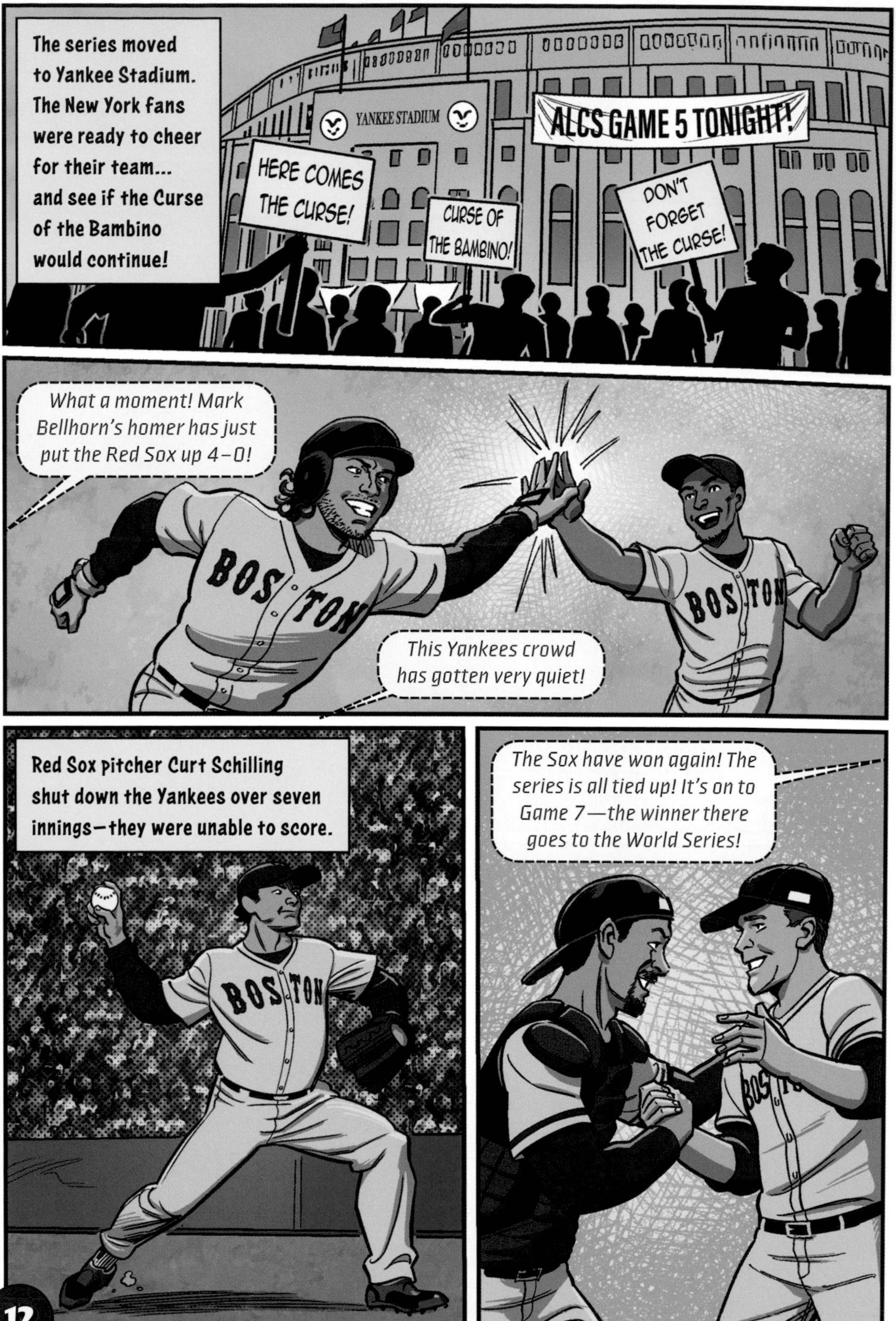
The series moved to Yankee Stadium. The New York fans were ready to cheer for their team... and see if the Curse of the Bambino would continue!
YANKEE STADIUM
ALCS GAME 5 TONIGHT!
HERE COMES THE CURSE!
CURSE OF THE BAMBINO!
DON'T FORGET THE CURSE!
What a moment! Mark Bellhorn's homer has just put the Red Sox up 4–0!
This Yankees crowd has gotten very quiet!
BOSTON
BOSTON
Red Sox pitcher Curt Schilling shut down the Yankees over seven innings—they were unable to score.
BOSTON
The Sox have won again! The series is all tied up! It's on to Game 7—the winner there goes to the World Series!

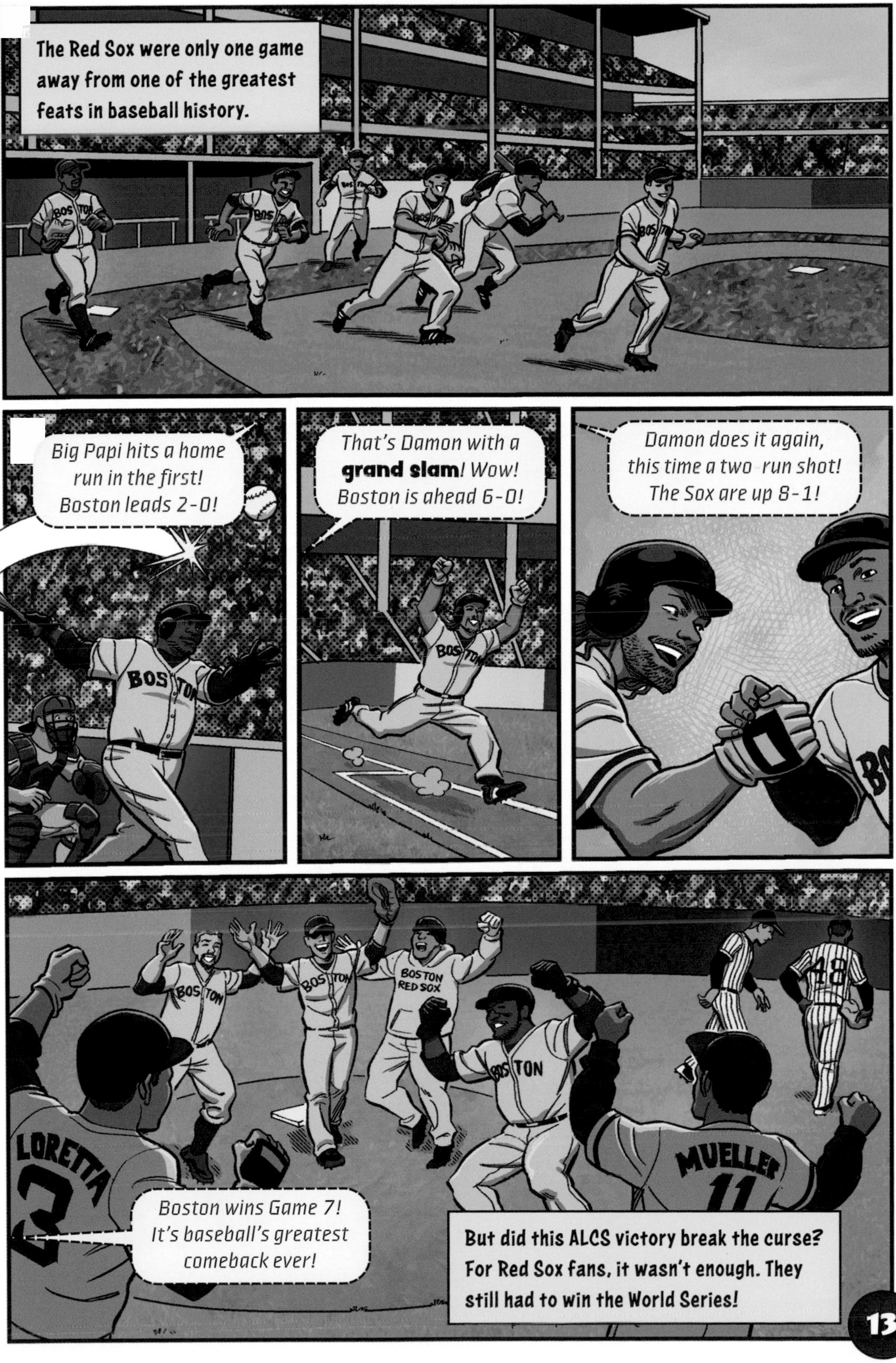
The Red Sox were only one game away from one of the greatest feats in baseball history.
BOSTON
Big Papi hits a home run in the first! Boston leads 2-0!
BOSTON
That's Damon with a **grand slam**! Wow! Boston is ahead 6-0!
BOSTON
Damon does it again, this time a two-run shot! The Sox are up 8-1!
BOSTON
BOSTON
BOSTON RED SOX
BOSTON
48
LORETTA
MUELLER
11
Boston wins Game 7! It's baseball's greatest comeback ever!
But did this ALCS victory break the curse? For Red Sox fans, it wasn't enough. They still had to win the World Series!

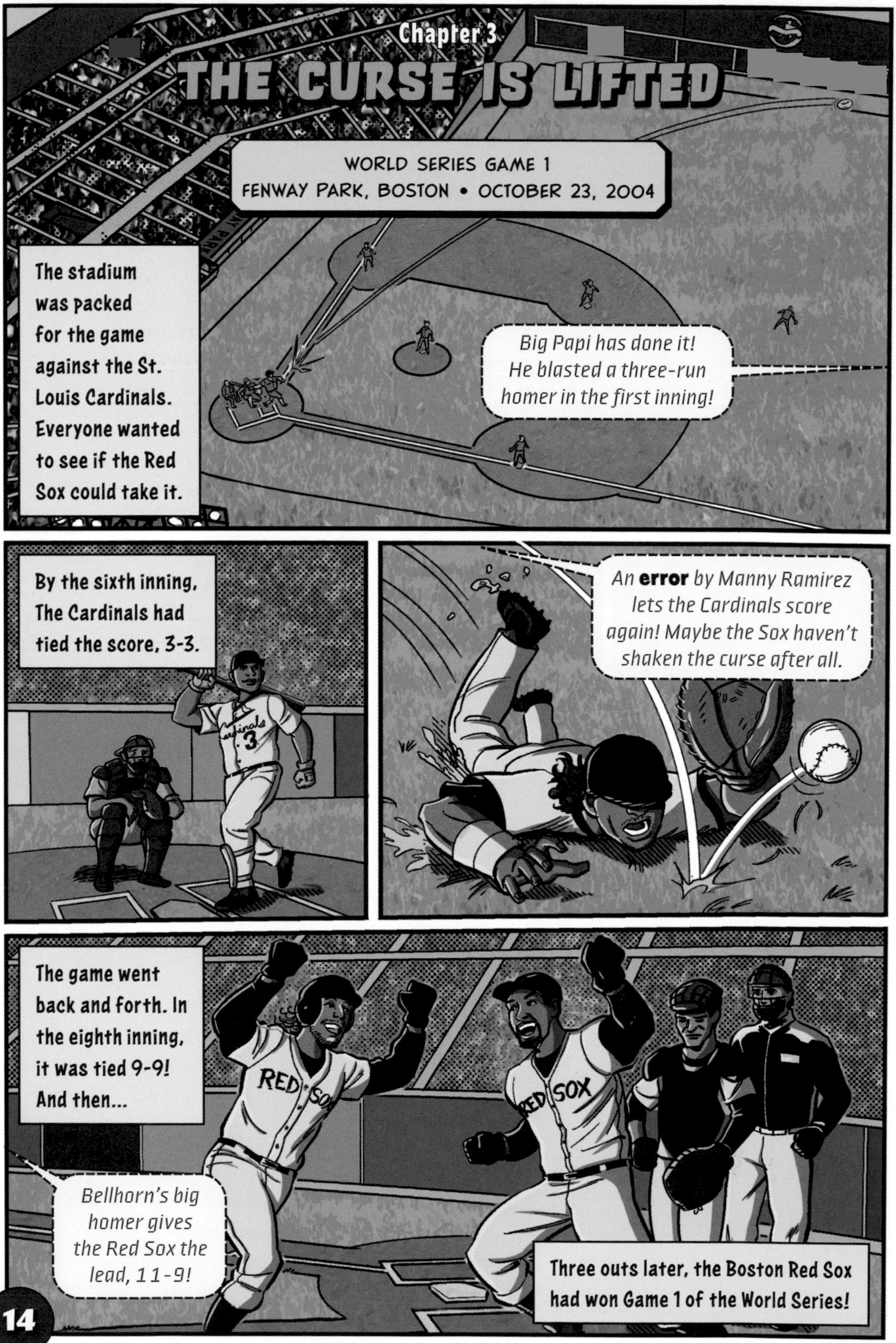
Chapter 3
THE CURSE IS LIFTED
WORLD SERIES GAME 1
FENWAY PARK, BOSTON • OCTOBER 23, 2004
The stadium was packed for the game against the St. Louis Cardinals. Everyone wanted to see if the Red Sox could take it.
Big Papi has done it! He blasted a three-run homer in the first inning!
By the sixth inning, The Cardinals had tied the score, 3-3.
Cardinals 3
An error by Manny Ramirez lets the Cardinals score again! Maybe the Sox haven't shaken the curse after all.
The game went back and forth. In the eighth inning, it was tied 9-9! And then...
RED SOX
RED SOX
Bellhorn's big homer gives the Red Sox the lead, 11-9!
Three outs later, the Boston Red Sox had won Game 1 of the World Series!

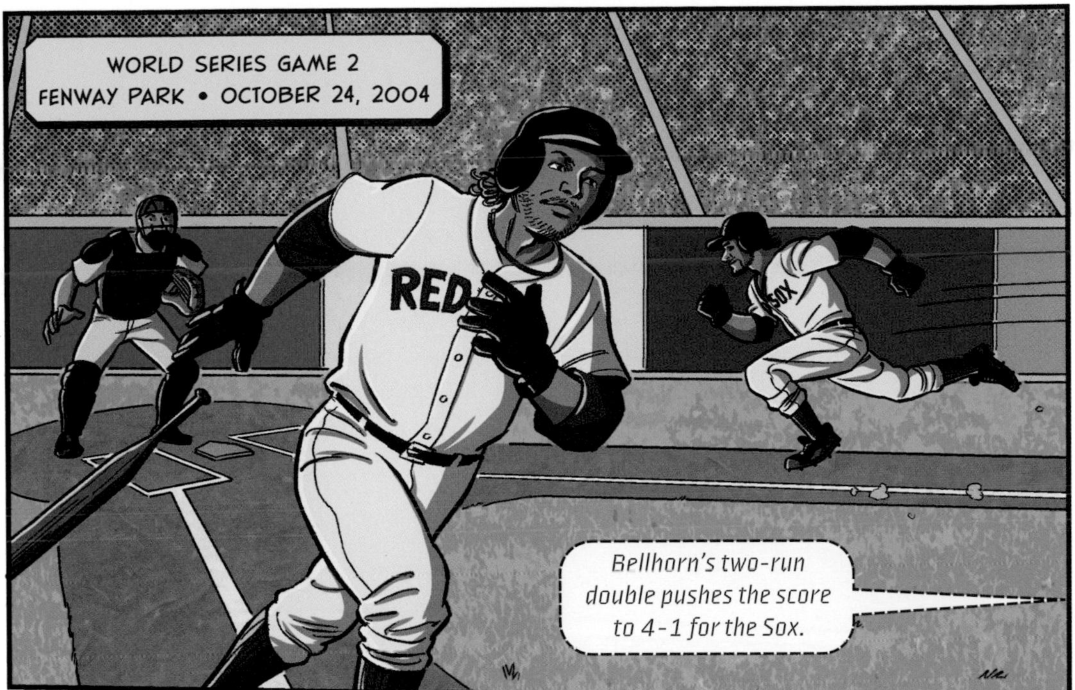
WORLD SERIES GAME 2
FENWAY PARK • OCTOBER 24, 2004
Bellhorn's two-run double pushes the score to 4-1 for the Sox.

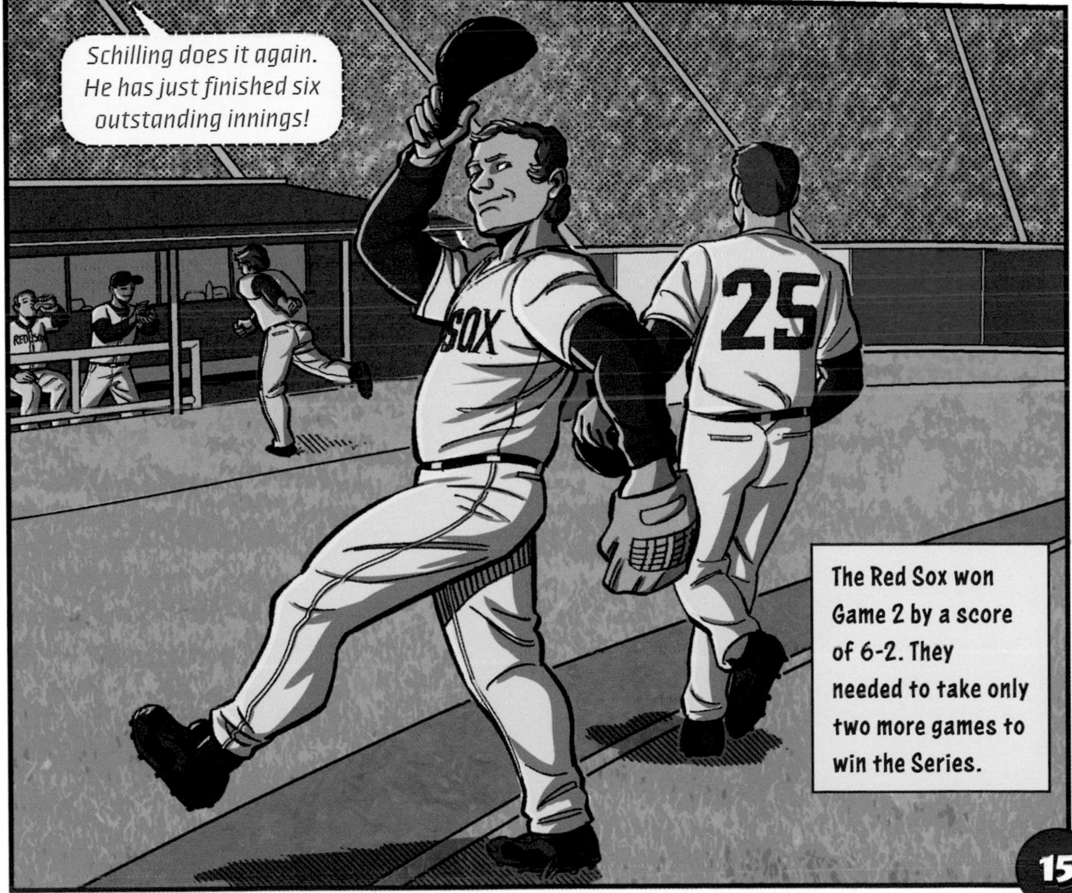
Schilling does it again. He has just finished six outstanding innings!
The Red Sox won Game 2 by a score of 6-2. They needed to take only two more games to win the Series.

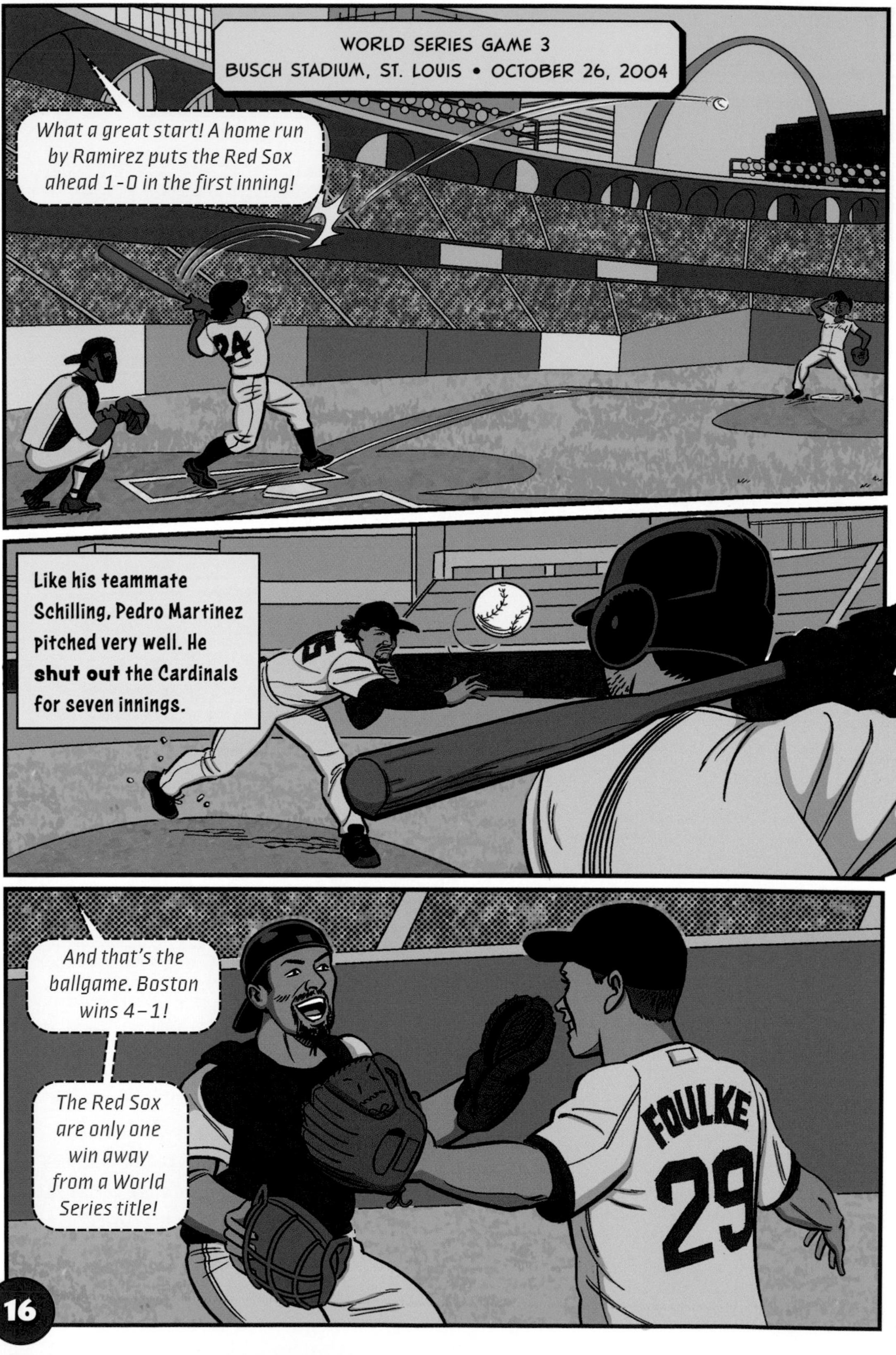
WORLD SERIES GAME 3
BUSCH STADIUM, ST. LOUIS • OCTOBER 26, 2004
What a great start! A home run by Ramirez puts the Red Sox ahead 1-0 in the first inning!
24
Like his teammate Schilling, Pedro Martinez pitched very well. He **shut out** the Cardinals for seven innings.
And that's the ballgame. Boston wins 4–1!
The Red Sox are only one win away from a World Series title!
FOULKE
29

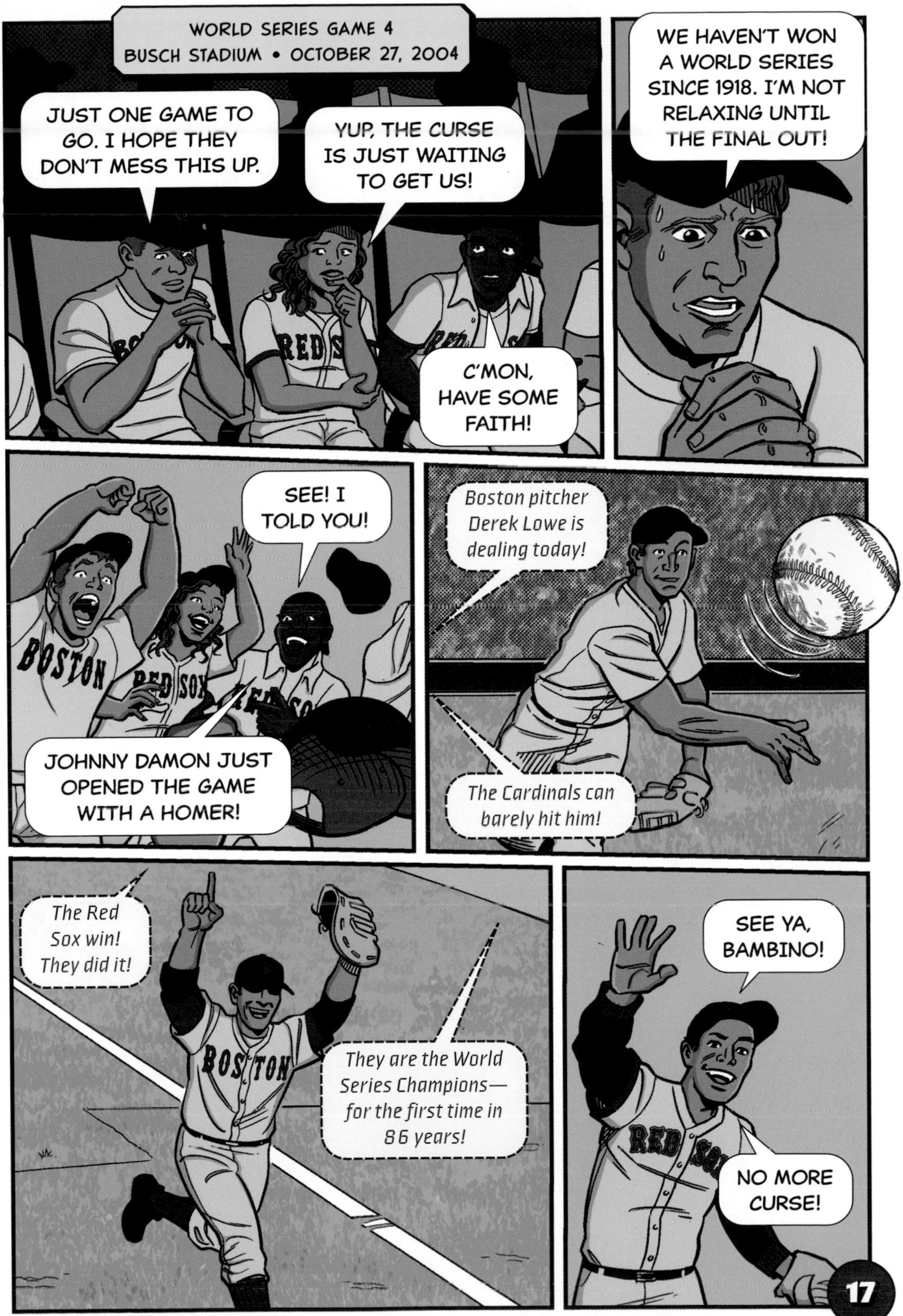
WORLD SERIES GAME 4
BUSCH STADIUM • OCTOBER 27, 2004
JUST ONE GAME TO GO. I HOPE THEY DON'T MESS THIS UP.
YUP, THE CURSE IS JUST WAITING TO GET US!
C'MON, HAVE SOME FAITH!
WE HAVEN'T WON A WORLD SERIES SINCE 1918. I'M NOT RELAXING UNTIL THE FINAL OUT!
SEE! I TOLD YOU!
JOHNNY DAMON JUST OPENED THE GAME WITH A HOMER!
Boston pitcher Derek Lowe is dealing today!
The Cardinals can barely hit him!
The Red Sox win! They did it!
They are the World Series Champions—for the first time in 86 years!
SEE YA, BAMBINO!
NO MORE CURSE!

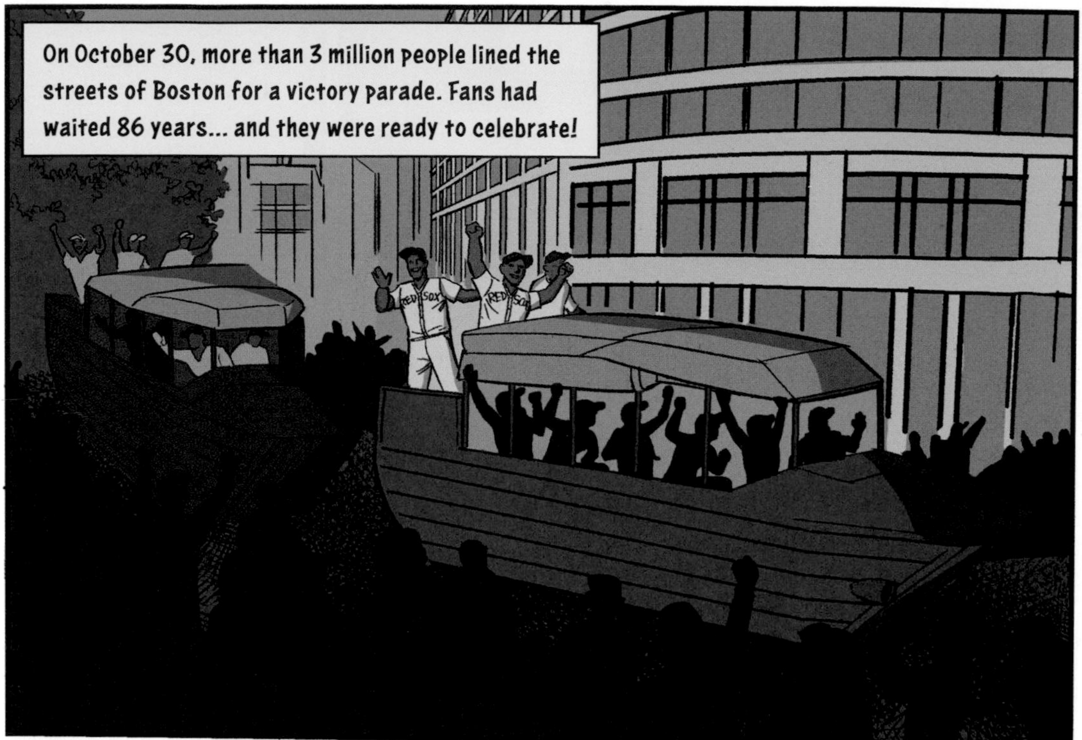
On October 30, more than 3 million people lined the streets of Boston for a victory parade. Fans had waited 86 years... and they were ready to celebrate!

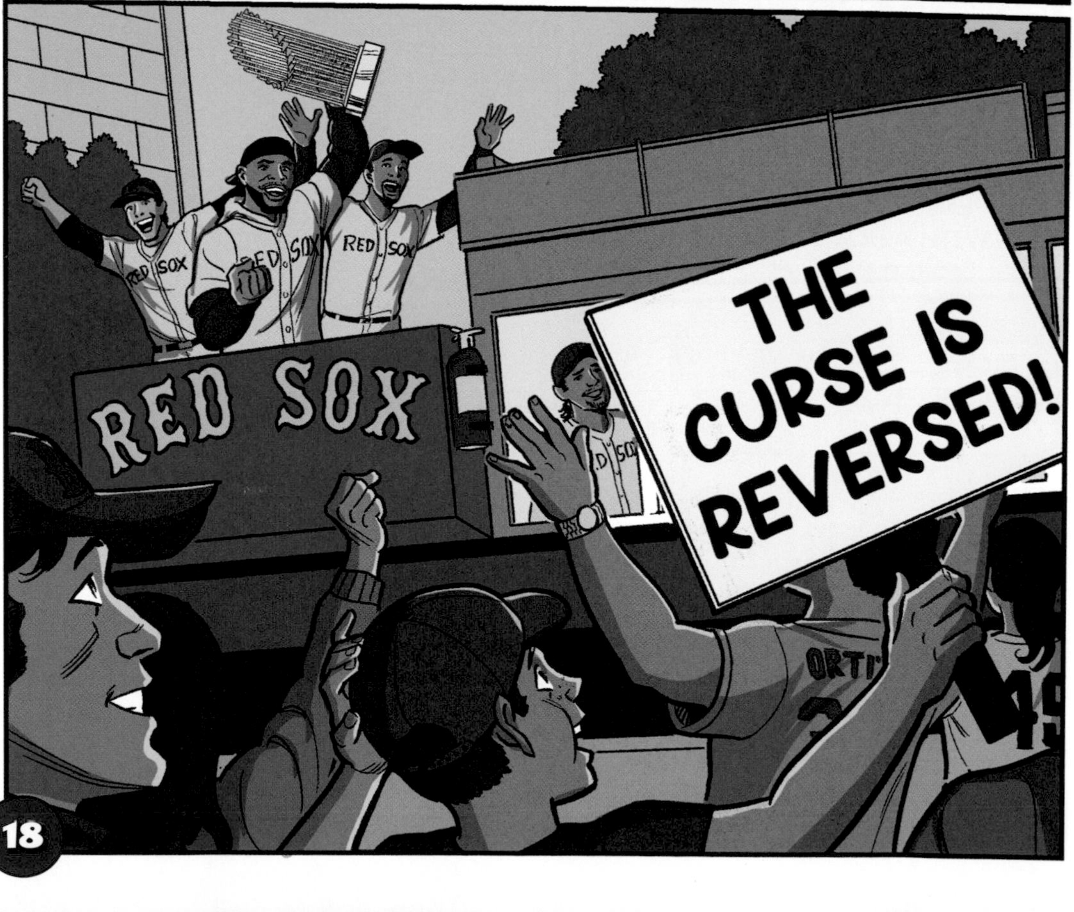
RED SOX
THE CURSE IS REVERSED!

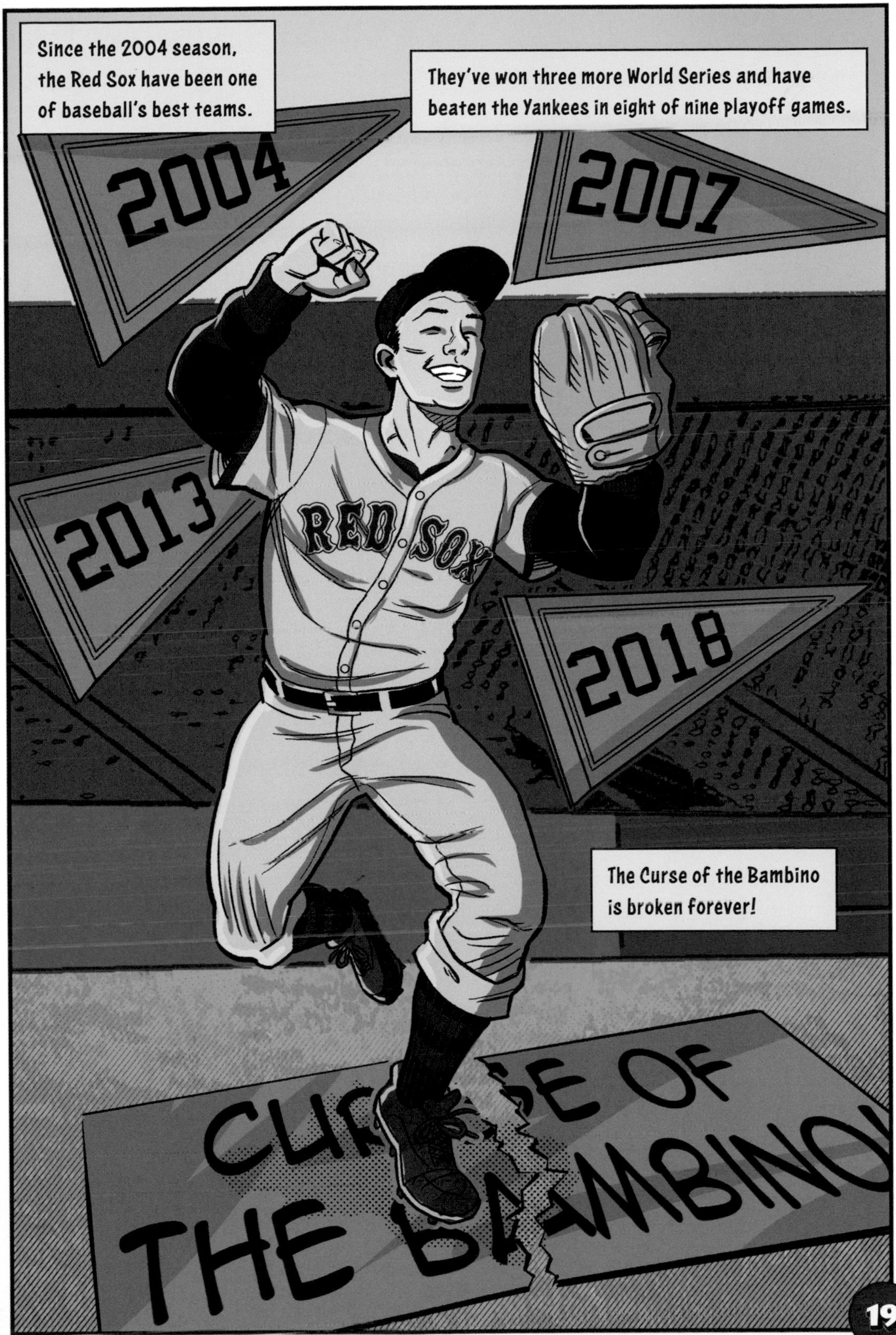
Since the 2004 season, the Red Sox have been one of baseball's best teams.
They've won three more World Series and have beaten the Yankees in eight of nine playoff games.
2004
2007
RED SOX
2013
2018
The Curse of the Bambino is broken forever!

WORLD SERIES HISTORY

The World Series determines the champions of Major League Baseball. The best team from the American League plays the top National League team in a best-of-seven series.

- The first World Series was played in 1903. The team from Boston, then called the Americans, beat the Pittsburgh Pirates in a best-of-nine series. The series switched to best-of-seven in 1922.

- The World Series has been held every year since 1905—except for 1994, when a players' strike ended the season early.

- The American League's New York Yankees have won the most World Series. The St. Louis Cardinals hold the National League record.

- The Red Sox run of 86 years between World Series wins was not the longest. In 2016, the Chicago Cubs won the team's first World Series in 108 years, breaking what Chicago fans called The Curse of the Billy Goat.

- The longest stretch without a World Series title now belongs to the Cleveland Guardians, who last won in 1948.

- Through 2022, six teams have still never won a World Series. They are the Colorado Rockies, Milwaukee Brewers, Seattle Mariners, San Diego Padres, Tampa Bay Rays, and Texas Rangers.

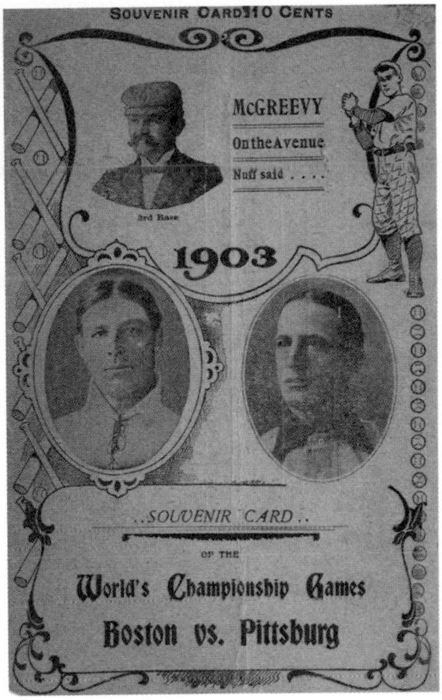
SOUVENIR CARD 10 CENTS
McGREEVY
OntheAvenue
Nuff said . . . .
3rd Base
1903
..SOUVENIR CARD..
OF THE
World's Championship Games
Boston vs. Pittsburg

The first World Series, in 1903, started the championship tradition in baseball.

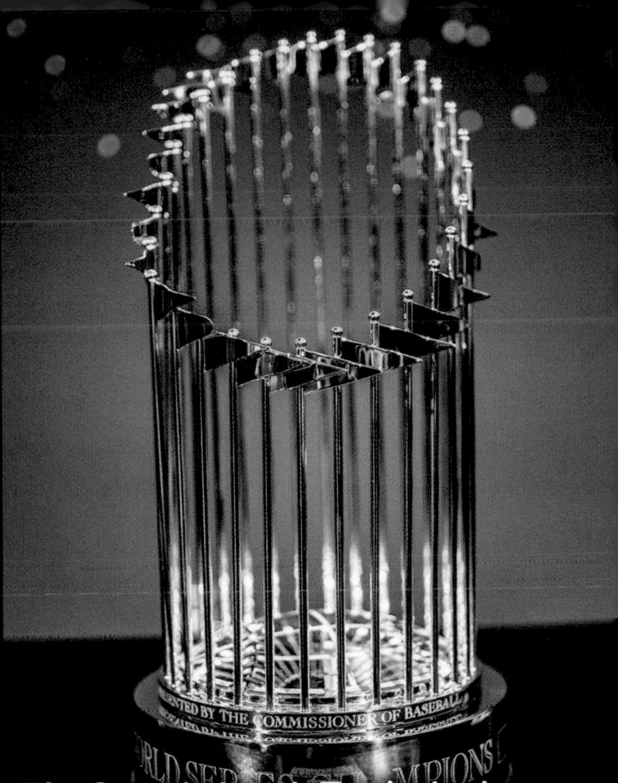
TED BY THE COMMISSIONER OF BASEBALL

The Commissioner's Trophy is given to the World Series winning team.

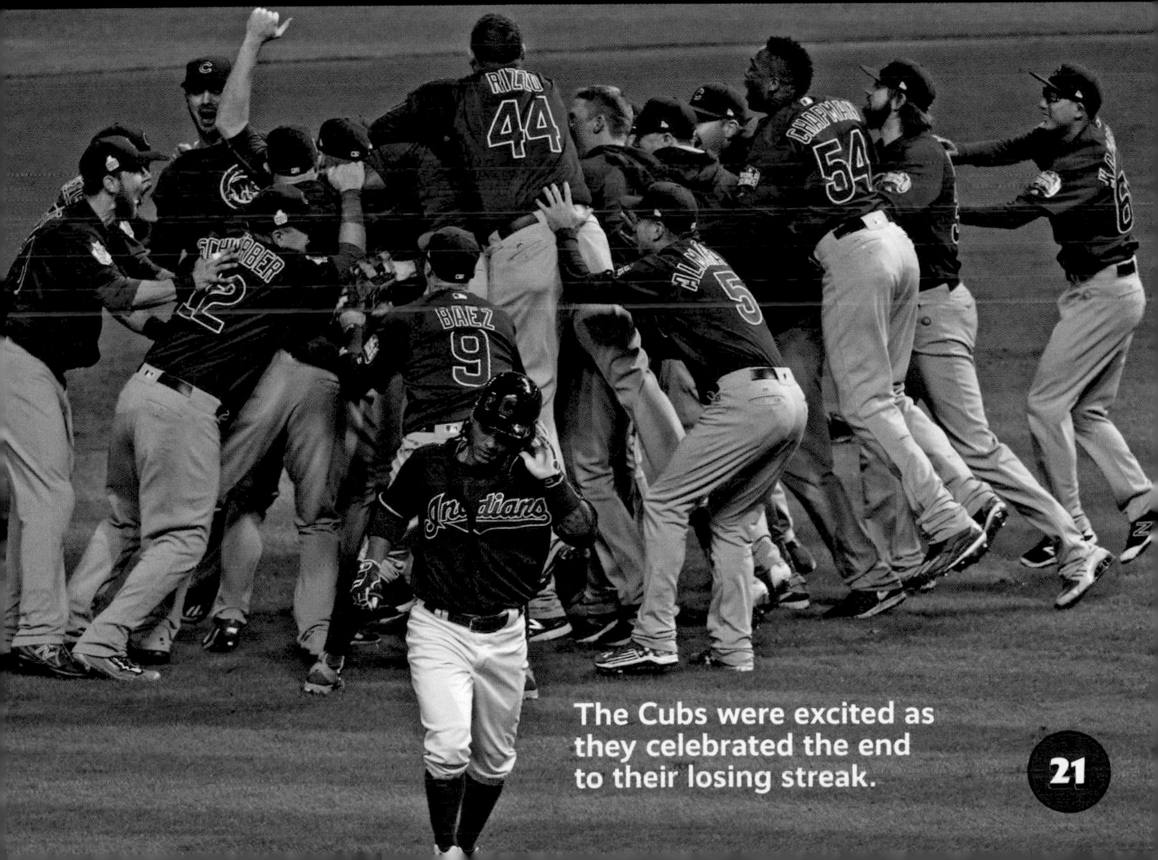
RIZZO
44
CHAPMAN
54
SCHWARBER
12
BAEZ
9
Indians

The Cubs were excited as they celebrated the end to their losing streak.

OTHER SPORTS CURSES

Madden Curse

One of the most popular football video games features a star player on the box. Strangely, many players given the honor were soon set to fall! It happened to Garrison Hearst in 1999 and Shaun Alexander in 2006. Peyton Hillis never had another good season after he appeared in 2012, and even the great Tom Brady lost the Super Bowl after he was on the 2018 cover!

Magazine Mayhem

It is considered an honor to be on the cover of *Sports Illustrated* magazine. But for years, some wondered if it was also a curse! The 1987 Cleveland baseball team was declared the best on the magazine's cover—then it lost 101 games. The Buffalo Bills made the cover before the 1992 Super Bowl and lost, too. Tennis star Serena Williams was on a 2015 cover and failed to clinch the title at the U.S. Open the same week.

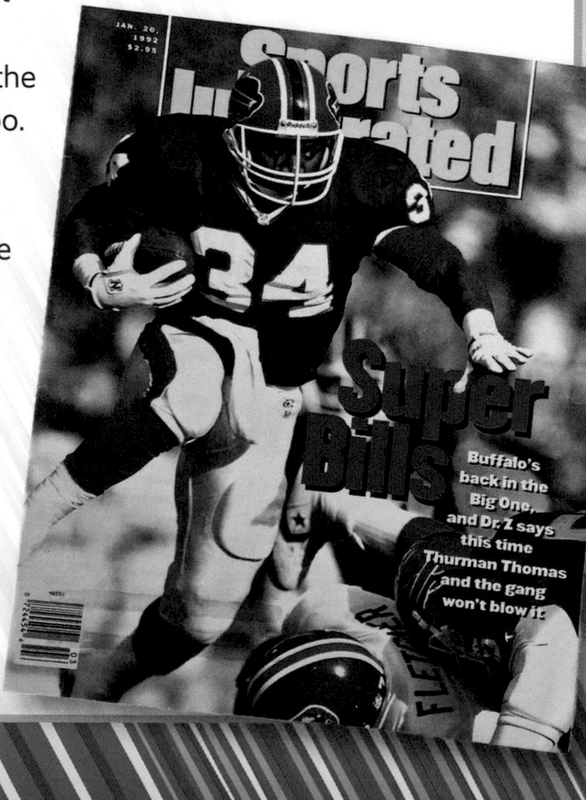
JAN. 20, 1992 $2.95
Sports Illustrated
Super Bills
Buffalo's back in the Big One, and Dr. Z says this time Thurman Thomas and the gang won't blow it
FLETCHER

The Buffalo Bills lost the Super Bowl after this cover was published!

GLOSSARY

double a hit on which the batter makes it to second base

error a fielding mistake that allows a hitter to reach base

extra innings additional rounds played in a game if the score is tied after nine innings

grand slam a home run hit when there were players on each base

homer slang for a home run; when the batter hits the ball out of the field of play

jinxed thought to be affected by bad luck

RBI short for run batted in; a stat that shows a batter got a hit that let a teammate score

rival a team's or player's fiercest regular opponent

shut out prevented the other team from scoring

singles hits where the batter reaches first base

steal run safely to the next base while the pitcher throws to home plate

traded sent away from one team to another

INDEX

READ MORE

Coleman, Ted. *Boston Red Sox All-Time Greats (MLB All-Time Greats).* Mendota Heights, MN: North Star Editions, 2022.

Fishman, Jon M. *Inside the Boston Red Sox (Super Sports Teams).* Minneapolis: Lerner Publications, 2022.

Smith, Elliott. *Baseball's Greatest Myths and Legends.* North Mankato, MN: Capstone Press, 2023.

LEARN MORE ONLINE

1. Go to **www.factsurfer.com** or scan the QR code below.
2. Enter **"Curse of the Bambino"** into the search box.
3. Click on the cover of this book to see a list of websites.